# The Human Condition

From the Bland-Lee Lecture Series
Delivered at Clark University
1979

# The Human Condition

*An Ecological and Historical View*

William H. McNeill

Princeton University Press
Princeton, New Jersey

Copyright © 1980 by Princeton University Press
Published by Princeton University Press, Princeton, New Jersey
In the United Kingdom: Princeton University Press, Guildford, Surrey

Printed in the United States of America by Princeton
University Press, Princeton, New Jersey


*Library of Congress Cataloging in Publication Data*

McNeill, William Hardy, 1917-
The human condition.

(Bland-Lee lecture series delivered at Clark University, 1979)
Includes index.
1.  Civilization—Addresses, essays, lectures.
2.  Human ecology—Addresses, essays, lectures.
I.  Title.    II.   Series: Chester Bland—Dwight E. Lee
lectures in history.
CB69.M33      304.2      80-7547
ISBN 0-691-05317-0

# Contents

# Preface

A university promotes scholarship less through the leisure it confers upon faculty and students than through the routines of classroom performance that require student and teacher to have something to say at a fixed point in time, ready or not. By compelling initial formulations of a given subject matter in this way, ideas are literally forced into existence, to wither or flourish under subsequent examination as the case may be.

The Bland-Lee lectures at Clark University partake of this tradition. The lecturer is free to choose his theme but has to have something to say at the appointed time, however incomplete his research or however imperfect his preparation. Without that compulsion, this essay would never have been written.

The text as actually delivered in September 1978 has been subsequently revised and (slightly) expanded, largely in response to criticisms and suggestions coming from friends and colleagues who read the first draft. The most helpful of these include Robert McC. Adams, Albert O. Hirschman, Arcadius Kahan, Donald McCloskey, Daniel Pipes, Hugh Scogin, and Edward Tenner. Although I have not always accepted their advice nor explored all the paths they recommended to me, the balance and (I trust) the persuasiveness of the essay that follows has been significantly improved thanks to their suggestions. Nevertheless, I thought it best to stick to the main lines of argument and assertion presented on the occasion itself, since anything else would distort the record and might, by multiplying examples and modifying generalizations to take fuller account of historical complexity, actually deprive the exercise of most of its value as a conspectus of the human past.

I owe a special debt to Professor George Billias who, as chairman of the Department of History at Clark University, acted as my host in Worcester, and to Professor Theodore von Laue who provoked the invitation in the first place, and reacted to what I had to say both sensitively and perceptively.

*Chicago, 12 October 1979*

I

# Microparasitism, Macroparasitism, and the Urban Transmutation

Although it is absurd to try to distill the human adventure on earth into the narrow space of two lectures, I propose to do just that. The absurd, after all, pushes us beyond the borders of ordinary discourse; and any intellectual discipline—not least history—needs every so often to examine the framework of understanding within which detailed researches and ordinary teaching are conducted. By trying to look at all of the human past in an exceedingly narrow compass, we will be forced to think about the really major landmarks—to consider, so to speak, the geological structures underlying details of the historical landscape. Even if my notions fail to persuade you, still this adventure into rash generalization may make you more conscious of how small-scale historical knowledge fits into, and derives part of its meaning from, the overall picture we have inherited from our forerunners.

The traditional framework within which the human adventure on earth has been studied in my lifetime has been about as follows. The human past fell into two main segments: prehistory and history, with the invention of writing marking the boundary. Prehistory divided into the Old Stone Age and the New Stone Age, followed by the Chalcolithic, Bronze, and Iron ages; history in turn passed through ancient, medieval, and modern periods.

[3]

On the face of things, this is a strangely discordant set of terms to apply to our past. Prehistoric periodization depended on the survival of materials from which tools and weapons were made—blithely leaving out the wood and other perishables that must have constituted a large part of the actual tool kit. On the other hand, the tripartite division of history rested originally on a very refined literary taste, being the invention of Italian humanists who believed they had inaugurated the modern age by reviving Ciceronian Latin and who deplored and defined the Middle Ages as a time when correct Latin had been forgotten.

To be sure, other meanings were subsequently poured into both classification systems. In the 1940s, V. Gordon Childe, for example, asked what uses defined ancient tool shapes and materials, and thus produced a quasi-Marxist evolution from hunting and gathering (Old Stone Age), to food producing (New Stone Age), to the urban age (Bronze Age and the entire historic period that followed).

Being older, the Italian humanists' division of history between medieval and modern has experienced rather more variegated and drastic reinterpretation. Early in the nineteenth century, for example, Leopold von Ranke organized the epochs of history in terms of interstate relations. Hence the Medieval Age began when the Roman Empire fell, and modern times started in 1494 when trans-Alpine powers eclipsed the effective sovereignty of the Italian city states. English learning usually preferred to pin modernity upon the European oceanic discoveries (1492 and all that), whereas the prophetic vision of Karl Marx defined ancient, medieval, and modern in terms of prevalent forms of labor—slave, serf, and wage.

More recently, subsections within modern times

have begun to assume greater importance for many historians, eclipsing or threatening to eclipse the older tripartite division of history. This elaboration got under way in the 1880s when Arnold Toynbee, uncle of the more famous Arnold J. Toynbee, invented the Industrial Revolution. It neatly coincided with the reign of King George III (1760-1820) for the simple reason that Toynbee had been hired at Oxford to teach a course about the history of that reign. Subsequently, other historians discovered a commercial revolution of the sixteenth century, and Fernand Braudel relocated it in the seventeenth century by emphasizing the geographic shift from Mediterranean to northern economic primacy in Europe in the 1630s. Simultaneously, and perhaps in imitation of the prehistorians, a multiplicity of technological eras have begun to decorate the pages of economic historians—the age of coal and iron, of electricity and chemicals, of atomic reactors and electronics, et cetera.

More recently, in the 1960s, it became fashionable to assert that contemporary conditions were so unprecedented that historical experience had become irrelevant. For such minds, various typologies setting up antitheses between traditional and modern societies justified a brisk dismissal of the premodern human past from any further consideration. Since they usually located the horizon of modernity in the nineteenth or twentieth centuries, the great majority of humanity's historical experience was excluded from these efforts to understand our own age.

Needless to say, I deplore the effort to dissociate humanity's deeper past from the contemporary encounter with the world. Yet a usable past must be intelligible; and it seems clear, even from my hasty remarks here, that we suffer from much confusion when it comes to any general mapping of the human condition through time. These lectures will add to the confusion by attempting to bring ecological ideas and terminology to bear. More specifically, I propose to look for shifting patterns of microparasitism and macroparasitism, treating them as twin variables that profoundly affected and continue to affect human life.

What I mean by microparasitism is, I hope, familiar enough already. The term refers to the metabolic activities of minute organisms that compete with human beings for food. They do so partly by invading the tissues of things we eat. By getting there first, microparasites can obviously forestall human efforts to capture energy from that food. Wheat rusts, animal murrains, and, more loosely, the depredations of insects and rats in human storehouses are instances of this kind of microparasitism.

Organisms can also invade human bodies and feed upon our tissues directly. Sometimes such invasions produce no obvious ill effect; often, however, sickness or death result. The impact of lethal and debilitating disease on human numbers, vigor, and ideas about the nature of things has been considerable. Encounters with microparasites—varying from individual to individual, from time to time, and from place to place in quite drastic fashion—constitute an ever present fact of biological life. Microparasitism, in short, constituted and continues to constitute a sort of nether millstone, perpetually abrading human efforts to assure individual and collective survival.

My use of the term macroparasitism, is, I must confess, less straightforward. From the time when our remote ancestors became the most formidable hunters on the face of the earth, no other species has been capable of feeding regularly upon human bodies by killing and eating them. Yet this is the ordinary meaning of the word macroparasitism; and in its proper definition, therefore, macroparasitism has played a trivial role throughout all human history.

Yet there is a metaphorical sense, it seems to me, in which one may say that when one man or group of men seize goods or compel services from other human beings, they are acting as an alien macroparasitic species acts, and they may therefore be called macroparasites by analogy. Certainly, most peasants who see someone else eat what they have produced or find themselves conscripted to work for another's benefit find that access to resources required for their own personal well-being has been reduced in proportion to the quantity of goods and services transferred by such transactions. When armed raiders break in upon a village of farmers, resemblance to the macroparasitism of one animal species on another is obvious enough. When it is tax or rent collectors who come to seize their share of the harvest, the resemblance is less obvious, since sudden death is not normally at stake in such situations. Still, if one thinks not of individuals but of biological populations, the dependence of a macroparasite on the survival of the plants or animals whose tissues it eats is similar to the dependence of the tax and rent consumer on the survival of tax and rent payers. Accordingly, customs and institutions that regulate the amount of tax and rent payments so as to allow the survival of the payers are analogous to the balances of nature that keep predators relatively few and their prey comparatively numerous—as, for instance, is true of lions and antelopes in the African game reserves.

I propose, therefore, to use the term macroparasitism to apply to exploitative relations among groups and classes of human beings. By doing so I think I will not do too much injustice to the exact ecological meaning of the word. Such a metaphorical usage has the advantage of inviting us to focus attention upon the human majority through time: those who after the invention of food production labored in the fields and paid over part of what they harvested to others who used such income for their own purposes. Only occasionally was there any palpable return to the tax and rent payer. On the other hand, protection from more ruthless, less experienced, alternative exploiters often did constitute an intangible though real quid pro quo.

If microparasitism may be likened to a nether millstone, grinding away at human populations through time, human-to-human macroparasitism has been almost as universal—an upper millstone, pressing heavily upon the majority of the human race. Between them, the two forms of parasitism usually tended to keep the peasant majority of civilized populations close to bare subsistence by systematically withdrawing resources from their control.

Though this may have been true on the average and over long enough periods of time, vast and destructive perturbations of macroparasitic-microparasitic balances often took place. Wars, epidemics, and mass migrations, which play so conspicuous a part in recorded history, amply attest to the precariousness of the ecological balances within which humanity has so far contrived to survive and even to flourish. For, despite all the catastrophes, human labor usually sufficed to repair the damage wrought by war and epidemic within a few generations. A pattern of unceasing fluctuation around an equilibrium point resulted. In principle (though not in practice) such a fluctuating equilibrium might endure for hundreds or even thousands of centuries, just as ecological equilibria do for other animals and plants.

To be sure, over a long enough time span, organic evolution alters plant and animal ecological relationships. On the foreshortened historical time scale, humanity's capacity to make discoveries and inventions does the same by sporadically tapping new forms of wealth. One invention is likely to provoke others. In that case, runaway change, echoing and reechoing within disturbed social and biological equilibria, may upset the balance between hosts and parasites for centuries at a time. In this way, human numbers and skills have repeatedly crossed previously unattainable thresholds. But always in the deeper past, a discernible tendency towards stabilization within new limits seems recognizable as macroparasitic-microparasitic balances reasserted their capacity to restrict and restrain human existence. Perhaps in a long enough time perspective, the industrial expansion of recent centuries will also conform to this pattern. New wealth, however abundant it seems, may not suffice to annul parasitism in human relations, despite what democratic theories of equality assume will, or ought to be, the case.

Yet however plausible this dismal view of the human condition may be, I do not mean to assert that it is a self-evident fact of life. On the contrary, mutuality is also a reality among human beings, and trade relationships, whereby both parties gain tangible advantage from the transaction, are as much a part of the historic record as are exploitation and lopsided taking. To be sure, trade and market-regulated production seem to have been of limited importance in the early stages of civilized history. For centuries, exchanges of goods and services, which were freely and willingly entered into by the parties concerned, flickered on and off, being perpetually liable to forcible interruption. Raiders from afar and rulers close at hand were both perennially tempted to confiscate rather than to buy; and when they confiscated, trade relations and voluntary production for market sale weakened or even disappeared entirely for a while. But market behavior always tended to take root anew because of the mutual advantages inherent in exchange of goods coming from diverse parts of the earth or produced by diversely skilled individuals. Little by little the scale and importance of mutually advantageous trade and manufacture for sale at freely negotiated prices increased. Thereby the direct clash of interest between exploited and exploiter was muted and sometimes even transcended.

How completely macroparasitic exploitation can be checked in the future seems to me an open question. So is the related question of how completely human skills can banish infectious disease or defeat rival forms of life that feed on human foods. Enormous and unexpected changes in these balances have occurred in the past; it is unlikely that infrangible limits in either direction will be attained in our time. Whatever catastrophes may lie ahead, the processes that have given humankind dominion over the face of the earth are not at an end, even if the two millstones of micro- and macroparasitism continue to grind. To identify times and occasions when systematic changes in these balances occurred will be the aim of these lectures.

I suppose that the first landmark of human ecological history was the advance of our remotest ancestors to the apex of the food chain. This was almost surely a result of the acquisition of language and of the superior coordination of human behavior that language allowed. Knowledge and skill could begin to accumulate when words allowed more precise discrimination of meaningful aspects of the natural environment, whether food or foe, tool or toy. No less important was the possibility of more exact cooperation in the hunt by agreeing on a plan ahead of time. Language also enormously facilitated the transmission of any useful new discovery or invention to subsequent generations. In the long run, accumulation of skills and knowledge that resulted from this capacity transformed humanity's place in the natural order.

The first fully human hunters and gatherers found themselves living in tropical Africa, surrounded by a very tight web of life. Africa's ecology included (and continues to include) a dense array of microparasites that had evolved with humanity itself. They were so adjusted to the human presence that any notable increase in human numbers promptly provoked a sharp intensification of infection and infestation.[1] Together with limitations on the availability of food, tropical microparasites sufficed to keep our remote ancestors relatively rare in the balance of nature.

The next landmark is no less a matter of speculative reconstruction, for it involved human penetration of colder and dryer zones of the earth, where most of the microparasites that limit human life in sub-Saharan Africa could not survive. Here the key invention was the use of clothes to maintain a tropical

[1] How powerful such natural microparasites could be in limiting human life is evidenced by the survival into the twentieth century of big game animals in east Africa in those landscapes where tsetse flies infect cattle and human intruders with lethal sleeping sickness. Malaria also put similar, if somewhat less drastic, limitations on human life in Africa until very recently.

microenvironment next to the almost hairless skin we all inherit from our cradleland. A bearskin on the back, together with the domestication of fire—a skill acquired close to human beginnings—allowed survival in freezing temperatures; and when sewing and tailoring were invented to improve the fit between animal furs and the human frame, even Arctic lands became penetrable by ancient hunters. This allowed a rapid expansion of human populations around the globe.

A few microparasites probably accompanied humanity in its grand dispersal: yaws, for example, could pass from skin to skin without ever leaving the warmth of the human body. But most tropical microorganisms could not fend off lethal cold as humans had learned to do. Hunting and gathering bands that penetrated temperate zones therefore left behind nearly all of the microorganisms that kept human numbers in balance with other forms of life in the African cradleland.

Humanity's first global population boom presumably ensued, wreaking serious disturbance to pre-existing ecological balances among large-bodied animals in temperate and sub-Arctic lands and throughout the New World. Skilled hunters able to penetrate new regions of the earth must have had an easy time killing large and unwary game animals—at least to begin with. Some scholars believe that the Pleistocene disappearance of hundreds of species of such animals, especially in the Americas, was due to reckless overkill by newly arrived human hunting bands whose numbers were no longer adequately restrained by tropical microparasites.[2]

---

[2] This interpretation of Pleistocene die-offs is not universally accepted. Climatic changes incident to the most recent advance and withdrawal of

Whether or not human hunters were the principal agents in the destruction of woolly mammoths and scores of other big animals, it seems clear that as these creatures disappeared, human communities accustomed to feeding upon them faced a severe crisis. It was met by intensified gathering—for example, by resort to the collection of shellfish along tidal shores, as is attested by some impressive shell middens in Europe. In several different parts of the earth, however, intensified gathering changed over into food production. Human beings learned ways of altering natural landscapes by deliberate action so as to increase the area in which a given food plant could grow. Whenever and wherever such actions became successful enough to provide a major part of the year's nutrition, a new way of life set in.

Methods of cultivation and the species of food plants human communities came to depend upon varied greatly. But the general idea of increasing the supply of food by altering natural landscapes, holding back weeds (i.e., competing plants without food value to humans), and increasing the abundance of a few desired kinds of plants was everywhere the same. It seems also to be true that efforts along these lines began at approximately the same time, even though results were sometimes delayed, as in the Americas, where far-reaching changes in the genetics of maize were required before the new patterns of cultivation could produce really large amounts of human food.

Whenever human beings succeeded in establishing a productive form of agriculture (with or without

---

the northern ice sheet may have mattered more. Human dispersal coincided with sharp climatic change, and it is a mistake to try to separate the influence of the one from that of the other in upsetting older ecological balances.

domestication of animals), the increase in population and the change in habit of life that food production brought with it increased the importance of micro-parasitism. Human actions aimed at producing a uniform stand of a single kind of plant offered an enlarged scope to all the insects, fungi, and viruses that were natural parasites of the plant in question. Thus, the more successful human farmers were in establishing a uniform plant population in their fields, the more vulnerable they became to losses from infections of this kind. In addition, food harvested and stored for use throughout the year became vulnerable to another array of parasites: rats and mice, insects, molds, and the like.

But humans could see their animal and insect competitors. Intelligence then often circumvented disaster, for example, by discovering ways to make storage jars proof against insects and mice. Even fungi and viruses could sometimes be fended off. Conditions of moisture and temperature conducive to the propagation of such forms of life could be—at least sometimes—both observed and subsequently avoided or minimized by appropriate human actions. But every deliberate alteration of natural life balances required a never-ending battle against "weed" species, ever ready to compete with human consumers as parasites upon the plants that human actions had made abnormally abundant in the balance of nature.

Parallel to this intensified struggle against competitors for the food humans hoped to consume themselves was an intensification of infections within human bodies. Communities that remained in the same location for years on end became vulnerable to a cluster of infections that enter the human body

[14]

through the mouth and are excreted with the faeces. Hunters perpetually on the move are seldom exposed to the anal-oral path of infection, while villagers living in proximity to their own faeces year after year become fair game for dysenteries and the like that are propagated from host to host in this way. The drinking of contaminated water was, after all, an everyday practice until 130 years ago, because human senses, unaided by the microscope, could not detect bacterial contamination.

The shift to food production permitted a second surge in human population, since a landscape given over to grain fields can support many times as many human beings as the same landscape used only for hunting and the gathering of wild foods. Still, there were limits to the amount of land that could be made into fields in every case, and before long the restraining force of intensified microparasitism also made itself felt. In the Near East, where information about the transition to food production is far greater than elsewhere, a leveling off in population density seems to have set in within two or three millennia of the first beginnings of agriculture. Frontier villages continued to multiply as farmers penetrated new regions as far afield as North Africa, Europe, and India. But in the initial heartland of the Near East, after about 5000 B.C. a potentially stable adaptation for humanity in its newly won ecological niche as engineer of the plant kingdom may plausibly be discerned from what remains a sketchy archaeological sampling of neolithic village sites. In other parts of the earth, too little is known to suggest a similar rhythm of initial expansion and subsequent stabilization of skills and numbers, though on a priori grounds it seems probable.

Nevertheless, the earliest village pattern of agriculture did not endure indefinitely. In the sixth millennium B.C., new and much more productive patterns of cultivation were inaugurated along the banks of streams flowing into the Tigris-Euphrates River. Two inventions were critical: irrigation, which brought water to growing crops as needed, thus assuring heavy yields; and the plow, which allowed field workers to keep at least four times as much land in tillage as was possible when only human muscles had been harnessed to the task. Plowing also made permanent cultivation of the same fields possible. Weeds could be controlled by fallowing, that is, by the practice of leaving some fields empty in order to destroy weeds by plowing the land during the growing season. Killing off competing species in this way created an ecological vacuum and did so easily and cheaply. In the next year, grain sown in such ground yielded abundant harvests, especially if the area was also watered artificially. Disasters were not completely banished: rust or blight on the grain or a flood to destroy the growing crop was still possible. But that sort of thing was unusual. In most years, the harvest richly rewarded the effort expended in its production.

Thus, by keeping twice as much land under the plow as was needed for the year's food, and by seeding only half of this land each season, a fully sessile agriculture arose in the Tigris-Euphrates valley, whereas in earlier times the only way neolithic cultivators had been able to escape weed infestation had been to abandon old fields after a few years' cultivation and carve new ones from the forest by the technique known as slash and burn. Plowing and irrigation obviously allowed far more intensive agricultural use of land than slash and burn cultivation had done. On the other hand, the gain carried its own nemesis, for fully sessile agricultural villages were also liable to new and intensified forms of parasitism.

Consider macroparasitism first. The fact that farmers could count on regular and abundant harvests made them capable of supporting others than themselves, if those others could find a way of persuading or compelling them to hand over part of their harvest. This did indeed occur between 4000 and 3000 B.C. in the Tigris-Euphrates flood plain. With the definition of customary patterns for transferring food from those who produced it to persons who no longer had to till the ground in order to eat, new sorts of social diversity became possible. Skills could accumulate as full-time specialists devoted their ingenuity to old and new tasks. The resultant highly skilled societies we commonly call civilized to distinguish them from simpler, more uniform human communities. Cities, where specialized elites clustered, were the hallmark of civilization.

No doubt, if tax and rent collectors pressed too heavily on those who worked in the fields, the option of flight remained. But in practice this was a costly alternative. It was rare indeed that a fleeing farmer could expect to find a place where he could raise a crop in the next season, starting from raw land. And to go without food other than what could be found in the wild for a whole year was impractical. Hence the high yield and dependability of irrigation plowing tied farmers to the land quite effectually and made such populations easy targets for tax and rent collectors. Civilization and the differentiation of occupational skills and routines that characterizes civilization depended on this elementary fact. And human society in its civilized form came to be fundamentally divided between hosts (the food producers) and parasites (those who ate without themselves working in the fields).

To be sure, it is not clear that the new relationship was especially burdensome to food producers at first. As long as a regular routine of work in the fields produced a surplus of grain over and above what the cultivator and his family could themselves consume in the course of the year, to part with the unneeded portion was no great loss. In return, the priests who managed the earliest irrigation societies assured good relations with the gods—no small matter, after all, in a world in which divine displeasure could bring swift disaster in the form of devastating floods or some other natural catastrophe. The planning and building of new irrigation projects and other public works— temples primarily—also fell under the jurisdiction of priestly managers and, when skillfully carried through, added to the total wealth and splendor of the society in a direct and obvious way. Hence the initial relationship between food producers and food consumers may have been symbiotic, involving relatively little loss to the peasant majority. But the statistical facts that would support or contradict this hypothesis are irrecoverable, and it is also possible that harsher exploitative relationships asserted themselves from the very beginning of civilized history.

Three aspects of this third major mutation of human life patterns seem worth comment here. First, the occupational specialization that permitted the rapid elaboration of skills thereby intensified the ecological upheaval that human actions imposed upon the natural web of life. From its inception, civilization acted upon its environment, altering and changing what had been there before in accord with the will of an increasingly skilled, powerful, and numerous population in the fertile plains. For example, timber, building stone, metals, and a long list of rare and precious commodities could only be found at a distance from the river flood plains, where the rich alluvium covered the subsoil and the climate would not allow large trees to grow. To bring such commodities from afar required improvements in transportation: wheeled vehicles, sailing ships, and the human organization needed to cut, quarry, or in other ways prepare and then transport goods across hundreds of miles. This meant that the civilization of the flood plains disturbed preexisting ecological patterns far and wide, imposing, or seeking to impose, complementary though often sharply contrasting patterns of behavior on peoples round about.

This side of the urban transmutation of human society is quite familiar, and I need not elaborate upon it further. A second aspect of urbanism—a marked intensification of microparasitism—is less familiar, however. Irrigation, for example, exposed cultivators to waterborne parasites, most notably the organism that completes its life cycle by moving between snails and men through fresh water, causing human schistosomiasis. Sewage and water supply problems, already significant for neolithic villagers, increased with the size of settlement, so that the anal-oral path of infection also carried an intensified traffic as cities came into being. Even more significant for the long-range future of human populations was the fact that when civilized communities achieved a sufficient size and density, viruses that pass from human to human via airborne droplets found it possible to survive indefinitely.

Such infections—smallpox, measles, whooping

cough, and the like—almost certainly became human diseases by transfer from animal herd populations. When they do not kill their host, these infections provoke long-lasting immunity reactions in the bloodstream. Hence if a virus is to survive indefinitely, it must always be able to find new and previously uninfected individuals, so that the chain of virus generations will not be interrupted. Only large human populations allow this: in recent times, for example, measles required a community of over 450,000 persons in order to survive. Obviously, birthrates and the custom of sending children to school affect the way a disease like measles was propagated in our time: still, so high a figure suggests how precarious survival of these viral infections must have been initially. Clearly, such an infection could only exist on a permanent basis among civilized societies where human populations were comparatively dense and communications nets far-flung.

Adding such viral infections to intensified anal-oral infections and to those infections transmitted to human populations via alternative hosts, whether insect or otherwise, obviously increased the microparasitic burden civilized populations had to carry. In short, organic evolution was catching up with humanity, weaving a new web of life around enlarged human numbers as a substitute for the African tropical network that had once restrained human populations so effectually.

There was, however, an ironical side effect. Disease-experienced populations in densely inhabited civilized centers acquired a notable epidemiological advantage vis-à-vis isolated, disease-inexperienced peoples. When newly inaugurated, contact between civilized populations and such isolated human communities often resulted in the outbreak of massively lethal epidemics among the former isolates. The effect of such vulnerability was to break down the capacity of such communities to resist civilized encroachment. The remarkable fewness of civilizations and the relative homogeneity of massive civilized populations in such places as China, the Middle East, and Europe resulted in large measure from this epidemiological-sociological process—or so I argue in my book, *Plagues and Peoples*,[3] to which I refer you for a fuller development of this line of thought.

The third aspect of the urban transmutation to which I wish to draw attention is the metamorphosis of macroparasitism that accompanied occupational specialization. Soon after cities first arose, the new skills that were generated by specialization and the relatively enormous wealth that resulted from irrigation and plowing made such cities worthwhile objects of attack by armed outsiders. Perhaps the initiation of armed aggression rested with the city folk, who probably took arms in hand when first they ventured forth to seek timber and metals and other needed goods. This, at any rate, is a plausible interpretation of what may lie behind the story of Gilgamesh as transmitted to us by much later (ca. 1800 B.C.) literary artists. But whether or not city dwellers were the first aggressors, it seems certain that during the third millennium B.C., raiding and plundering became an important feature of Mesopotamian life. Other civilizations in other parts of the earth seem also to have experienced a parallel shift from predominantly priestly to predominantly military management, whenever and wherever civilized skills created

[3] William H. McNeill, *Plagues and Peoples* (New York, 1976).

[21]

sufficient wealth to make raiding and warfare worthwhile.

Men preying upon other men thus began to create a new kind of macroparasitism, distinctive of civilization in much the same way that the viral dropletborne infections were also distinctive of civilization. Only a rich and differentiated society could sustain human-to-human macroparasitism by producing enough wealth to make its forcible seizure a viable, ongoing way of life for specialized warrior populations. Viruses could only survive when the density of human populations surpassed a critical threshold; warriors needed both a suitable number of potential subjects and a suitably advanced distribution of skills among them. Without numbers and skills, the long-term survival of a class that consumed without itself producing either the food or the arms its members required was impossible. Such a ruling class, therefore, was as much a hallmark of civilization as were the viral diseases. Poorer and more dispersed human communities simply could not sustain either form of parasite for long.

A warrior ruling class resembled viral infections in another way: a society capable of supporting their claims upon the body social became lethally formidable in contact with other, less differentiated communities. What viruses started, military specialists completed—defeating, demoralizing, and in general breaking down the autonomy and independence of border folk who, having come into contact with an expanding civilized society, ordinarily lost their separate identity as the price of survival.

Between an intensified microparasitism and this new style of civilized macroparasitism, therefore, it is safe to say that significant additional drains upon the resources available to peasant farming populations came into play during the first thousand years of Near Eastern civilized history. Clearly, the disturbance of older balances that human skills had created when the urban transmutation began was in process of correction, even though human capacity for fresh invention from time to time continued to disturb the equilibrium between civilized populations, productivity, microparasites, and macroparasites.

I do not intend to undertake the application of this scheme to the ups and downs of political and economic history in the ancient Near East or elsewhere, as this would require far larger compass than these two lectures provide. Let me merely remark, therefore, that the new exposure of human populations to micro- and macroparasitic invasions tended across time to move from sporadic epidemic to more nearly stable endemic forms. As far as microparasitic infection is concerned this is a familiar proposition. Adaptation between host and parasite always tends toward mutual accommodation, and in recent times expert observers have recorded in detail some striking examples of how accommodation proceeds when a new infection breaks in upon a previously inexperienced population.[4]

Viral herd diseases became diseases of childhood wherever human populations and communications

[4] The best introduction to this theme that I am acquainted with is Frank Fenner and F. N. Ratcliffe, *Myxomatosis* (Cambridge: Cambridge Univ. Press, 1965). This book describes in detail the way in which rabbit populations of Australia and Europe reacted to their encounter with a new and, to begin with, enormously lethal infection that had been deliberately introduced by human agents in hope of thereby reducing rabbit densities. Adaptation by the myxomatosis virus due to selective survival of less lethal strains and adaptation among rabbits for survival in face of the new infection combined to stabilize rabbit populations (at a much lower level than before) after about three years had passed.

nets attained sufficient density to maintain the infection on an enduring basis. Even though rates of lethality might remain high, human populations found it comparatively easy to replace young children who might die of smallpox or measles or other similar infections. Costs of such endemic exposure were far less than when the same disease visited a community only at long intervals—say once every thirty to fifty years—in which case every person who had been born since the infection had last been present was vulnerable. In such circumstances, death of parents and of the economically productive age groups was far more costly than an identical death rate spread evenly across time and confined to infants and young children. In such a fashion, then, infections could and did accommodate themselves to human populations, securing a more assured life cycle for the infectious organisms as well as for their human hosts. This is the way organic evolution works; and as childhood disease patterns established themselves, civilized concentrations of human populations became more securely adapted to their microparasitic environment.

A parallel evolution also occurred on the macroparasitic side. The major manifestation was the rise of imperial command structures. These became ever more elaborate and extensive from the time of the first recorded conqueror, Sargon of Akkad (ca. 2250 B.C.), to that of the Achaemenids, the Han, the Romans, and the Mauryans in the Old World, and of the Incas and Aztecs (building upon the work of their predecessors) in the New. In all parts of the civilized world, the key device facilitating the rise and consolidation of these imperial command structures was acceptance of the bureaucratic principle. By this I mean the way in which an individual appointed to office through some ritual act assumed a role that changed his behavior and that of persons around him in far-reaching and more or less predictable ways. Behavior changed because such an appointed official became a symbol of the sovereign ruler himself. In this way, sovereignty could be exercised at a distance and in the absence of the ruler, as long as officials and those around them accepted the roles that appointment (and replacement of one officeholder by another) implied.

Once government at a distance became feasible in this fashion, more stable patterns of contact between rulers and ruled made long-range advantage more apparent, while short-range considerations became less compelling than before. To put things in a nutshell: from the ruler's point of view, plunder became less attractive than taxes, and from the subject's side, a predictable tax payment became preferable to the enhanced risk of depredation that freedom from taxes and the absence of a powerful protector entailed.

The consequent accommodation between ruler and ruled was very like the accommodation between microparasite and host that endemic disease establishes. Custom and institutional forms defined an acceptable level of rent and tax payments—acceptable in the sense that in most years, when weather was normal and no external disaster intervened, customary levies were compatible with the survival of the tax and rent payers until the next season. One can, indeed, think of the relationship as a sticky market in protection costs. Too high a price for protection either killed off the tax and rent payers by leaving them too little for their own sustenance or persuaded them to flee to some other place where lower protection costs promised an easier life. On the other hand, too low a price for protection might allow an outside challenger to raid and plunder because the resources at the disposal of the imperial officials and military establishment were inadequate to drive intruders from the scene.

To be sure, there were enormous inefficiencies in all of the imperial command structures whose details are known to historians. In particular, local magnates and landholders commonly intercepted income from cultivators and weakened the power of central authorities by diverting resources to their own uses—only part of which were related to the protection of the rent payers. Yet feudal devolution of this kind was restrained by the fact that every civilized society confronted external rivals. In Eurasia, the most notable such rivals were bands of steppe cavalrymen, whose nomadic way of life fitted them for war and whose mobility allowed them to take advantage of any weakening of local defenses on the part of civilized rulers. Most of Eurasian political history, in fact, can be viewed as an unending fluctuation between imperial consolidation and feudal devolution, punctuated from time to time by epidemics of nomad invasion whenever the defenses of settled agricultural communities became insufficient to hold back armed raiders from the steppe.

The macroparasitic process, in other words, tended to seek an equilibrium point at which tax and rent payments transferred to the ruling classes sustained an armed establishment capable of repelling outside raiders, yet not so large as to require or permit its members to resort to plunder and rapine on their own account at the expense of the peasantry and of customary, constituted rent and tax collectors. When the optimal point was approximated, security of life for the producers and income for the rulers could both be maximized. But defining that optimum and maintaining it when defined was difficult indeed. Rulers and landowners were systematically advantaged by having superior force at their disposal. Countervailing this lopsidedness was the weight of custom, reinforced by religiously sanctioned general rules.

By a process of trial and error, perpetual interplay between armed force and the force of custom and religious injunction defined effective limits to rent and tax collection at a point that gave the producers a modest cushion against a year of bad crops. Only in this way could they survive the kinds of natural disasters that constantly afflicted farming communities. In a good year, surpluses retained in peasant hands could be converted into capital goods: tools, draught animals, clothing. In a bad year, cultivators often reached the verge of starvation, or died of hunger, in which case decades might pass before human numbers could recover.

Yet however important war and taxes may have been for civilized populations subjected to imperial command structures, epidemic disease was probably more important in cutting back population and wealth. This was, at any rate, true in the centuries and regions of the earth where approximate data can be found—that is, in early modern Europe and China. Yet even in the absence of quantifiable data, it seems certain that sporadic exposure to lethal diseases was very old among rural populations in contact with and subject to urban centers. Scattered populations in the hinterland could not sustain the endemic viral diseases of civilization. Instead they became liable to peaks of infection and heavy, abrupt die-off after years had passed without exposure to the disease in question, that is, after a long enough time for a sufficient number of vulnerable people to come into existence to support a new epidemic.

Obviously stability was never fully achieved, either in microparasitic or macroparasitic balances. Yet it seems plausible to suggest that shortly before the Christian era the kind of approximation to a stable state that I imputed to neolithic villagers before the rise of cities in the Near East can be detected within each of the civilizations that had sprung into existence in Eurasia by that time. The rise of the Roman and Han empires west and east was matched by the existence of comparable, if less well-known, imperial structures in the regions in between—in Mesopotamia, Iran, and India.

One can imagine this as constituting a sort of natural climax and end point of adaptations arising from the shift to agriculture as the principal basis of human existence. Increased human numbers, which food production occasioned, had found appropriate patterns of social organization, and the enlarged scope for micro- and macroparasitism had set limits to the further growth of human populations. Only along undeveloped frontiers—in southern China and India, or across the Eurasian steppe to the north, and in the forested zones of northwest Europe—was there much prospect for expansion. Each of these regions offered obstacles to agricultural settlement. The obstacles were partly climatic and technical. Plowing the steppe was a formidable task for light scratch plows, which were all that existed at that time, and northwest Europe was too wet for Mediterranean farming methods to work. In addition, epidemiological obstacles were also important, since south China, Southeast Asia, and south India, together with all of sub-

Saharan Africa, were infested with malarial and other parasites that made dense human occupation precarious, at least until such time as human labor was able to transform natural landscapes by improved drainage and the like so as to reduce exposure.

Yet even if such an hypothesis seems logically attractive, the path of historical development actually proved it false. What happened instead was that new patterns of human interaction began to affect societies and civilizations as transport and communication across Asia and the southern oceans assumed regular, organized forms. This became important from about the time of the Christian era, when caravans started to travel from China to Syria and back again, while ships connected Egypt with India and India with China through a series of segmented voyages.

A multitude of customary and technical breakthroughs were necessary to sustain this sort of long distance transport of men and goods. How to build and pay for a ship was only the beginning. Navigational know-how, crew discipline, security of passengers and their goods on board and in the ports along the way all had to achieve satisfactory definitions. For caravans, the rules of the road were at least as complicated. Safety lay in numbers, but keeping scores or hundreds of beasts of burden moving at the same pace for thousands of miles was no easy matter, especially since they had to be fed almost every day and if they carried their own fodder, useful payloads quickly diminished to the vanishing point.

Protection from robbers along the way was, of course, crucial both for ships and caravans. Indeed, long distance trade on a regular basis became possible only when constituted authorities en route all agreed that it was advantageous to allow goods and merchants to pass through territory they controlled, paying such fees for safe passage as the traffic would bear. Trade tolls could allow rulers access to a trickle (or even to a torrent) of wealth otherwise unattainable to them; but it took a long time for the possibilities of this sort of parasitism on commerce to become apparent, since everything depended on the scale of the transactions taking place. In the short run, high tolls—even outright confiscation—brought greater gain to local rulers. But, paradoxically, lower tolls might produce a larger total income by attracting more business. Finding an optimal level for assessing tolls on trade was presumably a matter of trial and error. The process must have worked in much the same way that customary rates for rent and tax collection set tolerable burdens upon local peasantries throughout the civilized world.

About the time of the Christian era, these technical, political, and sociological adjustments had attained such a degree of perfection as to allow long-distance trade to assume a new importance in human affairs. All the great civilizations of Eurasia came to be regularly connected with each other by shipping and by animal pack trains, and an expanded range of trade probes went out from civilized centers into barbarian lands that lay both north and south of the slender belt of dense agricultural settlement to which civilized forms of society were still confined.

Human historical relationships thereby began to assume a new scale—ecumenical rather than civilizational in scope. I would like to call the shift a "commercial transmutation," and treat its course and consequences as analogous to the urban transmutation that inaugurated the rise of civilizations. The urban transmutation of human society had begun between

4000 and 3000 B.C. and, as we have just seen, matured into imperial bureaucratic states and what I have termed "civilized" patterns of infection by about 1 B.C. The commercial transmutation, being a mere two thousand years old, has yet to arrive at any comparable climax equilibrium. It is unlikely to do so until some kind of world government emerges, for only a government extending completely around the globe seems capable of matching the commercial exchanges that have become so massive and important to everyday living in recent centuries.

Although human adjustments to the commercial transmutation are not yet complete, we can still hope to analyze its initial stages with the same broad brush I have used in discussing the impact of the urban transmutation that preceded it.

The first point that emerges from such a consideration is this: the initial impact of the commercial transmutation was epidemiologically disastrous, at least for the two extremes of the ecumene, Rome and China. Previously separate civilized disease pools flowed together. Viruses and other infectious organisms moved with ships and caravans across previously uncrossable distances. Relatively dense, previously unexposed populations thus became vulnerable to lethal infection on a hitherto unprecedented scale.

The result was registered in the Mediterranean world by the so-called Antonine plagues of the second century A.D. when, perhaps, measles and smallpox first broke in upon the population of the Roman empire. Drastic depopulation (up to one-third at first onset) and corresponding impoverishment ensued. Eventually, as one disease disaster followed another, the military, bureaucratic, and *rentier* drain upon the productive classes of the Mediterranean became insupportable, and the Roman empire disintegrated under barbarian pressure and internal disorganization. Very similar events occurred in China, where the Han empire also collapsed in the third century A.D., allowing barbarians to invade a depopulated landscape.

In the Middle Eastern lands and in India, no comparably drastic die-off from disease seems to have occurred, although records from those parts of the world are less well-preserved and have been less thoroughly studied than is the case for Rome and China. Imperial bureaucratic consolidation of those regions had been more precarious before the Christian era than at the extremes of the civilized world, perhaps because microparasitic burdens on the population were greater and allowed a smaller amount of resources to be concentrated in the hands of rulers and landlords.

Whether or not that was the case, the setback to wealth, population, and imperial bureaucratic administration that occurred in China and the Mediterranean lands inaugurated a thousand years of large-scale instability all across the Eurasian civilized world. To be sure, the initial disease disasters that arose from intensified travel across the breadth of the continent were in time counteracted by the diffusion of superior ideas and techniques that added to human wealth and power and probably also helped to stabilize civilized society. These travelled along the same paths as disease germs did, sometimes arriving sooner, sometimes taking root only later.

The most obvious instance of this process was the rise and dissemination of the great world religions—Christianity, Buddhism, Islam and Hinduism—as well as of less numerically successful rivals—Judaism, Manichaeism, and Zoroastrianism. Astrological and alchemical ideas also spread widely; so did devices like stirrups, wind and water mills, the abacus, and place notation for numbers. Religions of salvation clearly made life on earth more endurable for their adherents and sometimes may have cushioned collisions within society—insofar at least as the ethical prescriptions of the respective religions were able to modify and mollify human behavior. In this sense, their rise and spread was as useful to civilized society as was the propagation of water mills, horse collars, sternpost rudders, or any of the other superior techniques that originated or diffused more widely during the European Dark Ages.

At the same time, one must also admit that the appearance and spread of religions that commanded intense human loyalties and channeled aspirations toward a supernal realm introduced a new, or newly powerful, focus for human conflict as well. The righteousness with which Christians fought Moslems and with which Moslems attacked Hindu idolaters is too familiar to need emphasis here. Religious conviction embittered such collisions and probably made them more blood-spattered than would otherwise have been the case. Moreover, within a single society, when differences of opinion about salvation surged to the fore, civil strife was sometimes intensified by the belief that eternal salvation and damnation were at stake. This was true within Christendom, as the wars of the Reformation attest; it was equally true within Islam, as struggles between Shi'a and Sunni prove. Among Buddhists and Confucians, doctrinal differences never inspired comparable conflicts, although armed monks and angry Confucians sometimes did resort to military force in domestic broils.

[33]

Yet even though religions of salvation inspired or embittered some human conflicts in this fashion, it is arguable that for most of the people most of the time, the moral injunctions and the hope for a better future that the teachings of the higher religions inculcated conduced to survival. Had this not been the case, the new religions surely would not have spread and survived as they did.

More generally, it seems clear to me that all human ideas and techniques faced an intensified selection for their utility under the disturbed political-social conditions that the disease disasters of the first Christian centuries inaugurated; and by about the year 1000 A.D., one can perhaps assume that the resulting enhancement of civilized capacities—both for social order and productivity within, and for defense without (epidemiological as well as military)—had laid the groundwork for a new upsurge of wealth and power that slowly became manifest across the entire breadth of the Eurasian ecumene.

Prior to that time, two rival and not very well-reconciled principles struggled for control over the civilized populations of Eurasia. On the one hand, there was the command system of empire, capable of mobilizing goods and manpower for vast projects, whether of peace or war. On the other hand, there was the price system, capable also of mobilizing human and material resources as long as superior force was not brought to bear in such a way as to interrupt the exchange of goods and services. Rulers and men of the sword commonly lived in awkward symbiosis with merchants and men of the marketplace. This had been true from the beginnings of civilization; what was different in the initial stages of the commercial transmutation was that political-military power often came to depend in significant degree on materials and services supplied to the rulers by merchants who responded to pecuniary and market motives more readily and more efficiently than to bureaucratic command.

Merchants were, in fact, objects of very general disdain and moral opprobrium. Ordinary people toiling in the fields to produce a harvest year after year felt that a man who bought cheap and sold dear was fundamentally dishonest, since he added nothing to what he sold but nonetheless profited by raising its price. Most rulers concurred, even when they tolerated and protected cheating and chaffering merchants. The plain and fundamental fact was that merchants' behavior violated patterns of mutuality that prevailed within primary groupings, whether among simple village folk or amidst the grandeur of a royal court where hospitality and gift giving supplemented prowess in cementing relations between the ruler and his military followers.

To be sure, a skillful merchant could sometimes enter into the warriors' gift giving by offering precious possessions gratis to a local ruler in confident expectation of receiving even more generous gifts in return. Marco Polo, the jewel merchant, made his way across Asia in this manner; and, in general, it was in the steppe regions of Eurasia that this technique found its greatest scope. In Islamic lands, a far more stable and predictable alliance between merchants and warriors resulted from Mohammed's revelation and example. Mohammed (570-632) had been a merchant before Allah chose him as his messenger, and the city of Mecca in which he lived was an important trade center where the social leaders of the community were themselves merchants as well as warriors.

Mohammed united the nomad tribesmen of Arabia with city-based merchants under the banner of his revelation, and in succeeding generations, when the "True Believers" conquered vast agricultural regions of the Middle East and North Africa, the resulting alliance between warrior and trader remained firm. Yet I do not think that distrust of merchants disappeared from Islamic lands: rather the normal, underlying peasant dislike of tax and rent collectors merged into a parallel dislike for cheating traders. Among Christians and Confucians, as is well-known, overt condemnation of greed and price gouging entered the high literary tradition; Buddhists, so far as I know, remained doctrinally indifferent, although in practice Buddhism and merchant communities came to be closely interconnected everywhere north of the Himalayas.

Despite the accommodation to merchant manners and morals that Islam and Buddhism exhibited, I would argue that the Christian and Confucian condemnation of cheating in the marketplace was closer to majority (that is, peasant) opinion. Yet however morally dubious their behavior might be, if it were given sufficient scope, merchants, acting in response to perceived self-interest and known price differentials, could assemble and assort goods and services at lower cost than any bureaucratic command system could. The market could attract goods from afar, crossing political frontiers and ocean vastnesses in ways that no ruler could hope to do on the strength of his own word of command, no matter how emphatic. Even within a single jurisdiction, men who saw their personal self-interest tied up directly in the safe delivery of a particular consignment of goods from place to place commonly performed the task more efficiently than officials who had compulsory labor at their disposal. Hence whenever rulers and military classes tolerated merchants and refrained from taxing them so heavily or robbing them so often as to inhibit trade and commerce, new potentialities of economic production arising from regional specialization and economies of scale in manufacture could begin to show their capacity to increase human wealth.

The upshot remained very much in doubt until after 1000 A.D. Distrust, disdain, and dislike of merchants often cut back or destroyed trade linkages; raiding and migrations of barbarian peoples disrupted existing command and market systems alike. Yet command and market systems continually revived and at the same time competed against one another in regulating human behavior on a mass scale. Only after the year 1000 did the balance begin to tip perceptibly and in an enduring way in favor of an enlarged scope for market-regulated behavior. With that slow change in world balances the modern age, as I propose to define it, set in.

II

# Microparasitism, Macroparasitism, and the Commercial Transmutation

In my first lecture I traced the development of humanity to its achievement of a potentially stable pattern of life under conditions of civilization. By about 1 A.D., commands issued from a sovereign center and applied locally by bureaucratic agents of a distant ruler acting in uneasy collaboration with local landlords, chieftains, and other men of power could regulate and (more or less) safeguard the sorts of mutual dependency that urban specialization had called into being among populations living hundreds of miles apart from one another. Such territorially extensive states as the Han, Roman, Parthian, Mauryan, and Kushan empires may therefore be considered as constituting an institutionally adequate response to the novelties inherent in the urban transmutation that began about 4000 B.C in Mesopotamia.

It is noteworthy that similar state structures arose not just in the Old World but also in the New, beginning about 1000 years later. Amerindian social organization had indeed not passed beyond this level of organization at the time the Spaniards broke in upon the Aztec and Inca empires of Mexico and Peru, bringing them to an abrupt and catastrophic end. The apparent convergence of patterns of development in mutually isolated regions of the earth suggests that the evolution from priestly to military-bureaucratic management was not simply accidental. Instead it seems plausible to believe that the intensified human interdependence that had been induced by urban specialization needed a protective carapace. Bureaucratic command systems were the simplest way to meet that need, perpetuating into adulthood a childlike dependence on a superior's direction.

My second major point was that, beginning about 1 A.D., a new kind of transformation began to assert its power over human behavior in the Old World—a change I propose to call the "commercial transmutation." This refers to an enlarged commerce that began to link China with the Mediterranean and both with India soon after the Christian era. Long-distance trade of this kind responded mainly to market price differentials. Decisions and actions initiated by thousands of private persons affected the movement of caravans and ships—and determined what they would carry.

Of course, such decisions were also affected by bureaucratic commands. Governments were always good customers—for some goods they were the only customers. But insofar as trade moved across jurisdictional boundaries, the power of officials and rulers was checked by the unwillingness of merchants to buy or sell at prices that would not meet their costs and assure them a profit as well. Official acts that violated this principle—a compulsory purchase at less than market prices or outright confiscation—dried up trade very rapidly. The same applied to more local exchanges within a single state. Thus, insofar as rulers and their officials fixed prices at less than market levels—a policy especially prevalent in the grain trade—they inhibited the development of the private sector of the economy and perpetuated the command principle whereby men acted not of their own free will but in obedience to orders coming from someone above them in the political-social hierarchy.

Civilized societies for the next thousand years exhibited an uneasy and fluctuating combination of command and market-regulated behavior, with neither principle unambiguously in the ascendant. Clearly, in times and places where the market principle was at a minimum, human beings obeyed more readily, having no obvious alternative. Yet when communication improved, for whatever reason, so that information about price differentials between here and there became available, the possibility of gain through private trading became apparent; and in proportion as that possibility was actually acted on so that mutually advantageous exchanges multiplied, resistance to unqualified obedience to official commands mounted. In such circumstances, commands continued to be effective only where they reinforced and conformed to the price patterns established by private trade relations.

Always at the bottom of society, the peasant majority continued to respond mainly to command. Rent and tax payments were imposed on them from above: price had little or nothing to do with it. To begin with, trade in agricultural products was an affair of landlords, whose rents readily exceeded their capacity to consume food, making sale in exchange for imported rarities or city-made luxuries a very attractive proposition. Town-based merchants thus found natural allies in landlords. Both classes sought to withdraw resources from the control of bureaucratic officials in order to maximize their personal well-being and standard of living.

Officials, of course, were often landlords or closely associated with landlords, with the result that the opposition was far from clear-cut or conscious. But the possibility of and temptation towards subversion of the simple marshalling of human and material resources in response to words of command was implanted like a low-grade chronic infection in the tissues of imperial bureaucratic empires thanks to merchants' and landlords' mutual interest in expanding the private market. After about 1000 A.D. this chronic infection of the constituted public order took on new virulence and by degrees penetrated more and more of the body social throughout the civilized world. In the most severely affected regions, the market even reached out to envelop the peasantry at the very bottom of society.

Before this take-off became unambiguous, local ups and downs between market and command behavior could be quite sharp. In the Mediterranean world, for example, the high point for trade and market behavior came between about 300 B.C. and 100 A.D.— stimulated, in part, by the way in which Alexander of Macedon squandered the gold hoard Persian kings had accumulated across generations. The enlarged money supply lubricated commerce; so did the rise of commercially minded Greeks to high official positions in the Hellenistic monarchies. From its Eastern Mediterranean focus, trade and market behavior slopped over into the Indian Ocean and towards the western Mediterranean as well. And this expanding commercial network provided the principle impetus for the establishment of caravan and shipping links with distant China.

In the second and third centuries A.D. came disastrous disease, and the Roman government had to revert to taxation in kind because market behavior had withered so drastically that its lubricant, ready cash, had almost disappeared and could no longer provide a practical basis for support of the army and official-dom. Yet even in the worst of times, trade did not completely come to a halt, and commercial linkages with China and India remained sporadically alive.

In ensuing centuries, rebellion from within and raiding from the steppes frequently broke up imperial command structures in the Mediterranean and all across Eurasia. But the advantages of centralization for defense tended, no less persistently, to reestablish territorially extensive states. Moreover, such states sometimes drew an important part of their resources from tolls on trade. This was especially true in the arid zones of Asia, lying between Egypt and India (Arabia, Baluchistan) and between Mesopotamia and China (Iran, Turan, and Sinkiang). In these regions, local agricultural resources were slender, so that rents and taxes could not constitute an adequate basis of empire; trade income accordingly mattered more. Yet tolls on trade constituted a very precarious basis for state power because long-distance exchanges were persistently vulnerable to local violence anywhere along the way. Still, this type of commerce revived no less persistently whenever a modicum of public order and the policy of local rulers reduced the risks of moving precious goods to acceptable proportions.

The role of steppe nomads in this fluctuating bal-ance was critical. They conquered settled populations repeatedly; but when they could not raid with impu-nity they traded instead. This was because the steppe peoples' way of life made them peculiarly susceptible to trade. Their herds did not, of themselves, provide an optimal basis for human survival. But by offering animal products in exchange for grain, nomads could secure a much enhanced food supply compared to what they could enjoy by living solely on meat and milk. Plainly, more people could survive on the steppes and in the semidesert fringe lands that lay to the south of cultivable regions of Eurasia by giving up a biologically unneeded concentration of protein in their diet and substituting cheaper carbohydrates. Trade in a wide variety of other objects—weapons, slaves, jewels, information—attached itself to this basic pattern of exchange, which was, of course, no less advantageous to landlords and city folk in agricultural regions whose diet, if restricted to cereals, was likely to be short of protein.

The result was to create a loosely interacting continuum across the Eurasian steppe and in the desert fringe lands to the south of Middle Eastern and Mediterranean centers of civilization. These vast regions where nomadism, raiding war parties, and peaceable caravans all came to coexist linked the separate civilizations of the Old World more and more closely from the time when horseback riding first imparted a new mobility to steppe and desert dwellers (ninth century B.C.). The role of nomad peoples reached a climax in the thirteenth century A.D. when the empire of Genghis Khan gave political and military expression to the increasingly intimate symbiosis between Eurasian grasslands and grain fields.

Once patterns of protein-carbohydrate exchange became firmly established so that denser steppe populations could arise, the conditions of their lives quite literally required nomads to observe customs that protected traders from intolerable exactions. Each year survival depended on getting hold of enough grain to go round. Flocks and herds could carry themselves to market, but grain coming back had to move by caravan. Nomads thus readily occupied part

[46]

of their time as caravan personnel, being already familiar with the management of animals. Moving back and forth between their homelands in steppe and desert, on the one hand, and civilized centers of life, on the other, such personnel became thoroughly exposed to merchants' ideas and values. Familiarity with the charms of civilization therefore infiltrated the nomad world, bearing a thoroughly commercial tinge. Although Arabia in the age of Mohammed offers the most accessible example of this process, similar transformations were certainly underway simultaneously among all the diverse Turkish, Mongol, and Tungusic peoples of the northern steppe.

Whenever peaceable relations between grasslands and cropland broke down, raid replaced trade quite automatically. The alternative was imminent starvation for herdsmen who had become dependent on cereal food to expand their caloric intake far above the levels they could derive from their flocks and herds directly. The resulting waves of nomad invasion and conquest that played so large a role in the political history of Eurasia between 300 and 1300 A.D. therefore brought commercially experienced rulers to power. This was true even on the fringes of the civilized world where Viking raiders and Japanese pirates replaced nomad herdsmen as rivals to constituted public authority. But seafaring robbers depended on trade as intimately as nomads had come to do. Only through organized, peaceable exchanges could haphazard hauls of booty be converted into the array of commodities required to outfit ships and crews on an on-going basis, season after season.

Hence the political upheavals so characteristic of the so-called Dark Ages had the effect of making the rulers of the civilized portions of Eurasia far more familiar with, and attuned to, the values of the merchant class than had been true earlier. The spread of Islam is the most conspicuous instance of this change; the conquests of Genghis Khan had a comparable importance further east and north. But even before the Mongol empire gave political expression to the new interconnectedness of steppe and cultivated lands, the kneading of market-regulated behavior into the political command structures of Eurasia achieved a critical breakthrough about the year 1000 A.D. From that time onwards, trade and market exchanges began to enlarge their scope generation after generation in what proved to be a decisive fashion.

The key change probably began in China. Under the Sung dynasty (960-1279 A.D., the Celestial empire developed a closely articulated exchange economy. China's shift from a command to a market-directed economy was, of course, gradual. The arrival of Buddhist monks, and of traders from Central Asia associated with Buddhism, constituted one critical input, beginning as early as the third century A.D. Another factor was the official decision in 780 to allow conversion of tax income from kind to money payments. Probably most basic of all was the artificial improvement of internal water transport, making movement of goods within China relatively cheap. The great landmark of this process was the completion in 611 of the Grand Canal, connecting the Yangtse and the Yellow rivers. But many lesser engineering works were also necessary before a widely ramified internal communications system up and down the two great rivers of China came securely into existence.

The tax shift from collections in kind to money payments both registered and confirmed the change that came to China's economy. Although this conversion had begun on a small scale and by way of exception in the eighth century, it became predominant soon after 1000 A.D. As the shift to money taxes occurred, officials began to expend tax monies by entering the market and buying goods and services that the government found needful. They thereby returned cash to the private sector, lending the weight of their authority to the further diffusion of market behavior within Chinese society.

Thereupon, all the advantages of specialization that Adam Smith was later to analyze so persuasively began to exercise their dominion across the varied landscapes of the Chinese empire. As efficiency of production grew, so did wealth. The officials of the empire, in effect, discovered (rather to their surprise) that by refraining from interfering with market behavior the government could actually increase its effective command over goods and services. As long as the enhanced wealth created by the commercial integration of China's various regions was still new, and growth continued spontaneously, the political authorities were usually content to let well enough alone. They only intervened occasionally to check private accumulation of capital when flagrant price gouging or some other infraction of Confucian propriety seemed to call for such action. Indirect regulation of price levels by issuance of paper currency was part of Sung official policy, and officials specializing in fiscal management developed a rather sophisticated doctrine about the relation between prices, money, and metallic backing for the paper currency.

If all this seems strikingly modern, I can only say that it was. Indeed I propose to date the onset of modern times from the eleventh century, when this

[49]

transformation of the Chinese economy and society got firmly under way.

Its effects were not, of course, confined to the provinces that reverently obeyed the Celestial emperor's commands. Neighboring peoples also joined the trade network, coming in as tributaries and subordinates, at least according to Chinese court rituals. Caravan contacts with central and western Asia, the steppes, and India multiplied. Far more significant was the development of seaborne commerce. Ships, as seaworthy as any known to Europeans, sailed to Korea and Japan; others coasted southward to Indonesia, and by the close of the eleventh century direct voyaging to the Indian Ocean from the South China Sea became common.

The effect within this vast sea room was much the same as the effect of improved internal water communications had been within China proper: trade exchanges multiplied, technology diffused, and various kinds of regional specialization expanded total wealth production in coastal regions of eastern and southeastern Asia very substantially. The most important example of this process was the importation of early ripening rice into China proper from the south (by 1012). This permitted rice to grow on hillsides where the spring runoff only lasted a few weeks, thereby enormously increasing the food production of southern China. In well-watered lowlands, early ripening rice allowed double cropping, with equally spectacular results. This massive growth of agricultural productivity meant that tax and rent income from the peasantry expanded (especially in central and south China) *pari passu* with the intensification of mercantile and artisan activity. The older, fundamentally rural, articulation of Chinese society that was cen-

tered upon obedience to commands coming from social superiors therefore remained alive and well, and
the new commercial and industrial populations never
really challenged the primacy of China's traditional
ruling class.

Official capacity to intervene in the market remained unquestioned; and when, under the Mongols
(who conquered China between 1211 and 1279), economically more reckless managers came to power, a
runaway inflation upset the Sung pattern of indirect
governmental manipulation of market prices. Paper
money was thereby discredited in China for centuries. China's initial development towards large-
scale technology and capitalistic organization of trade
and industry also suffered crippling shocks, largely
through official purchases of strategically important
commodities at uneconomic prices. This began before the end of the Sung dynasty, and eventually
brought economic growth almost to a halt. Large-
scale private wealth survived only when associated
with such officially approved enterprises as tax farming—for example, management of the manufacture
and distribution of salt. Official actions thus stabilized
China's massive surge towards a market economy by
about 1500, just when western Europeans, reacting
more slowly to intensifying trade exchanges, entered
upon their modern, globe-girdling military and
commercial adventures.

I must admit that the spectacular economic boom
of Sung China did not have any obvious impact on
the Middle East. In that ancient center of trade and
commerce, Islam had already (from 632) encouraged
and sustained a substantial commercial development;
and it is probable that the warmer climate of the
eleventh through the thirteenth centuries, which im-

proved western European harvests and promoted that region's economic growth, brought damaging drought to Middle Eastern grain fields. At any rate, no sign of an economic boom of the kind that came to the Far East can be discerned in the Islamic heartland; and from the thirteenth century, if not before, Iraq began to suffer economic decline as irrigation canals went out of service.

One might perhaps view what happened in China between 1000 and 1500 as an application to the Far East of patterns of political and commercial symbiosis that were already age-old in the Middle East. The same was far more obviously true of western Europe.

Within the Mediterranean, a new vigor and efficiency of trade developed in the eleventh century when Italian ships took over the task of transporting goods from port to port. Simultaneously, Italians also took over Moslem (and Byzantine) legal regulation of business and details of commercial practices almost without modification. For several centuries, however, European commercial networks remained far less highly developed than those of China. Marco Polo's report of his travels (1271-1295) emphasized the massive scale of Chinese cities. His wonder at the size of everything in that country is evidence of how far the Chinese of the thirteenth century had outstripped the rest of the Eurasian ecumene.

Yet Europe eventually caught up. From the very modest levels of the eleventh century, trade conducted by Latin Christians tended to expand, despite cyclical ups and downs and despite the active distrust of market behavior and the ringing denunciations of usury that churchmen regularly voiced. As Chinese sea commerce began to unite Japan, Korea, and

Southeast Asia into a single market area, so, too, the advance of navigation (and some critical political acts) in Europe led to the merging of Mediterranean commerce with the commerce of the Black Sea to the east and of the Atlantic and Baltic to the west. The key date for the opening of the Black Sea was 1204, when Venetians and a motley company of crusaders captured Constantinople and opened the straits to their ships for the first time. The equivalent date for the opening of the Atlantic waters to Italian enterprise was 1290, when a Genoese buccaneer and businessman, Benedetto Zaccaria, defeated the Moslem authorities who had previously sealed the straits of Gibraltar to Christian shipping. Thereafter the wool trade of northwestern Europe could link up with the spice trade coming into the Mediterranean from the southeast, creating a growingly complex interdependence across very long sea distances and among numerous and diverse political structures.

Even though European commerce remained weaker and less massive than the exchanges sustaining the interregional integration that occurred under the roof of the Chinese imperial state, the fact that Far Western trade patterns ran across innumerable political boundaries gave market-oriented human behavior in Europe a decisive advantage compared to anything enjoyed by Chinese merchants and the producers who fed goods into the private trade nets of China. As we shall presently note in more detail, this was demonstrated in interesting and fateful fashion in the fifteenth century, when Chinese imperial authorities prohibited sea voyaging on the ground that it diverted valuable resources from the more urgent tasks of land defense against a threatening nomad power across the northwest frontier.

Perhaps it may be useful to distinguish two waves in the ecumenical upsurge of market-oriented behavior. One wave rested mainly on overland trade networks reaching from China to eastern Europe by northerly routes across the grassy steppes, as well as by the older oasis-hopping route of the classical Silk Road. This trade net sustained and was sustained by the Mongol empire that briefly brought China, Russia, and lands in between under one political roof. Italian commerce responded by developing Black Sea ports as a major exchange point with the caravan world to the east.

However, this linkage across Eurasia carried its special nemesis in the form of lethal outbreaks of bubonic plague. The arrival of the Black Death in Europe in 1347 is well known, and recent studies show that it took more than 130 years before European populations regained the levels they had attained before the new disease struck. The effect upon steppe populations was far more damaging because their grassy homeland became a permanent reservoir for the plague bacillus—or so I have argued in my book *Plagues and Peoples*[1] to which I should refer you for a fuller discussion of the evidence.

As had happened in the late classical age, when unfamiliar diseases wreaked havoc with population and wealth in the Roman and Chinese worlds, the political register of the die-offs resulting from bubonic exposure among nomads was the disruption of large state structures. The Mongol empire broke up into warring fragments, and the trade net across the steppes was never restored. Central Asia sank towards marginality, economically, politically, and cul-

---

[1] William H. McNeill, *Plagues and Peoples* (New York, 1976).

turally. This was because, in addition to the direct impoverishment due to population losses from disease, a new, second wave of commercial development propagated itself across the seaways with such vigor as to make resumption of overland transport uneconomic, even if local conditions had allowed the caravans to travel once again as freely as they had in Marco Polo's age.

Official Chinese expeditions into the Indian Ocean began on a truly imperial scale early in the fifteenth century, only to be withdrawn and permanently abandoned after 1430 as a result of orders from the imperial court in Peking. The enterprise of Chinese merchants operating from the southern coast could not prevail against official command. Resources, such as gunmetal, needed to equip oceangoing ships, were desired by the imperial majesty for its own uses far to the north; ship building was accordingly abandoned. China's chance to forestall the Portuguese in the Indian Ocean and Columbus in the Americas was thereby foreclosed, simply because the commercial classes of China remained so thoroughly subject to an imperial bureaucracy as to inhibit large-scale independent enterprise on their part.

In the Far West a different development occurred, as is well known. Portuguese ventures down the coast of Africa eventuated in the rounding of the Cape of Good Hope and the discovery of a sea route to India in 1499. Earlier in the decade, by seeking Cathay, Columbus found America and opened a new world to European enterprise. The familiar Commercial Revolution of the sixteenth century ensued, linking American production of gold and silver with European commerce and European commerce with the spices and other precious products of the Indian

Ocean. Eventually Japan and the south China coast also entered into the European-managed exchange pattern. Shift of the most active centers of European trade and manufacture from the Mediterranean to northwestern Europe soon followed—a shift completed only in the seventeenth century, with the rise of the English, Dutch, and French trade empires. As a result, the modern integration of the globe into a single market-regulated economy was already well under way by 1700.

Thus China's abdication was Europe's gain. Put another way, the demonstration of the power of the Chinese imperial command system to confine and redirect market-oriented behavior prevented China from taking an active part in the development of a global sea-trade network. Instead, Europeans took over; and their continued exploitation of the wealth-generating possibilities of such trade was sustained by the fact that no single political authority existed in Europe to redirect activity, as had happened in China.

By dominating long-distance sea trade, European merchants concentrated much new wealth in European cities. On top of this, the new regime of the seas provoked a growing primacy of the Far West over other civilizations of the earth on three distinct levels: ideational, microparasitic, and macroparasitic.

First of all, in intellectual matters, Europeans could afford to be curious about the newly apparent diversity of the earth. Since they controlled communications with alien peoples, they felt no immediate threat from the new contacts their seamanship opened up. Instead, any useful novelty that came to their attention could be considered, wondered at, and, if it seemed worthwhile, appropriated for their own use. A systematic openness to new thoughts resulted, whereas in other civilized regions of the earth, when the alien presence seemed menacing to any aspect of inherited values—as happened sooner or later in each case of cultural encounter—a defensive mentality asserted itself that sought to close out everything unfamiliar and dangerous to established verities. Such stubborn conservatism could not compete with the self-confident curiosity that sustained the rapid development of European skills and knowledge until they clearly outstripped all rivals—a situation generally achieved by the eighteenth century.

The circulation of ideas, in other words, took on a new pattern and velocity that was of special advantage to Europeans as a result of the growth of global trade networks. Precisely the same was true of the circulation of microparasites. Disease-experienced regions of the earth, where civilized densities of population and communications networks had already established high levels of immunity to a large number of microparasitic infections, suffered relatively little from the new seaborne contacts. To be sure, ports like London and Lisbon became notorious for their unhealthiness, and indeed periodic epidemics wreaked very great damage to city populations in Europe (and presumably elsewhere) between the fifteenth and eighteenth centuries. But as the frequency of such visitations increased, losses concentrated on younger and younger age groups. Within a couple of centuries, most lethal epidemic diseases became endemic, at least in the largest port centers, so that only infants and small children were likely to die of them. As upcountry trade linkages intensified, larger and larger hinterlands also became increasingly disease-experienced and less liable to suffer disastrous die-off of adult populations when some infection not encountered for a generation or more spread out from an urban bridgehead.

Hence, as infections became more and more homogenized throughout the civilized world, their demographic impact altered in such a way as to facilitate population growth. Children were relatively easy to replace; even high infant mortality rates could be counterbalanced by correspondingly high birth rates. On this basis, civilized populations began to grow whenever and wherever enhanced food production made such growth feasible. This trend became unmistakable sometime during the eighteenth century in both China and Europe; Indian populations probably followed the same curve, but it is unlikely that Middle Eastern communities did so. Perhaps this was because enlargement of food supplies in the Middle East was not as easily achieved as elsewhere, since none of the American food crops—maize, potatoes, sweet potatoes, and the rest—were well suited to the semiarid landscapes that predominate in the Middle East.

In previously isolated parts of the earth, however, the new microparasitic regime inaugurated by oceanic voyaging proved disastrous. Heavy die-off regularly resulted from contact with European and other civilized populations. In many parts of the earth—North America, Australia, southern Africa, Siberia—the effect was to empty or nearly empty fertile lands that thus became available for European settlement. Colonies of settlement—starting for the most part in the seventeenth century—enormously enhanced the expanse of ground available for European exploitation and reinforced European prosperity by supplying agricultural goods and raw materials on a rapidly expanding scale in exchange for manufactures issuing from European workshops.

These microparasitic and demographic responses to the new regime of the seas were matched by similarly drastic changes in macroparasitic patterns. First of all, the advantages that cavalrymen had enjoyed ever since the ninth century B.C. were largely nullified by the spread of gunpowder weapons. Steppe raiding became ineffectual against soldiers armed with guns—a fact that sealed the shift away from the steppe and towards the seacoasts as the critical frontier for all parts of the Eurasian civilized world.

It took a while for this transformation to become irreversible: it was not until the first half of the seventeenth century that the eclipse of steppe cavalry tactics became an accomplished fact. The Chinese and Russian empires were the two states that gained most from this shift of fortunes between agricultural and nomad war-making capacity. Accordingly, during the course of the seventeenth and eighteenth centuries, they expanded their landward frontiers across the interior of Asia until they fetched up against one another and inaugurated a series of clashes that have not yet reached definitive resolution.

More important in the short run was the diffusion of cannon, which occurred with the earliest arrival of European ships on the coasts of Asia. Here was a weapon that allowed its possessor to knock holes in castle walls within a few hours of its successful emplacement. By monopolizing control of big guns, a monarch could assure himself of hitherto unattainable superiority over local rivals. In case of quarrel, the *ultimo ratio regis* could come into play—after only a few months of delay—anywhere that existing means of transport would allow big guns to go.

The practical effect was the establishment of a series of what can properly be termed gunpowder empires, whose size and stability against rebellion from within was far greater than anything before possible. The consolidation of Japan under Hideyoshi (d. 1596) and the Tokugawa shoguns is the clearest example of how decisive gunpowder weapons could be in forwarding political consolidation. But the Ming empire in China (1369-1644) and its successor the Ching (1644-1912), no less than the Mughal empire of India (1526-1857) and the Ottoman empire of the eastern Mediterranean and adjacent parts of the Middle East (1453-1923) were other notable examples of the species. And so, for that matter, was Muscovy (1480-1917); while the Portuguese and Spanish overseas empires differed only in depending on cannon-carrying ships to unite the provinces with the capital.

In western Europe, however, the thrust towards the creation of a single political authority misfired. Despite his impressive dominions in Europe and the Americas, Emperor Charles V (1519-1556) failed to consolidate his power over Germany, much less to conquer France; his son, Philip II of Spain (1556-1598), could not even keep the Dutch under his control. Thus western Europe's political diversity survived the gunpowder revolution as happened nowhere else in the civilized world.

Why this should have been so is a matter deserving more careful consideration than I can give here. Technical factors certainly mattered. For example, Europe's precocious development of hard rock mining (compared to that of other civilizations), dating back at least to the eleventh century, meant that many different sources of gunmetal existed, so that no one ruler could easily monopolize access to the copper, tin, and zinc needed for casting big guns. More decisive still was the fact that in the first decades of the sixteenth century, ingenious Italian architects discovered that revetments of earth could protect stone walls from the destructive force of gunfire. By combining this with crossfire from heavily gunned bastions and a dry ditch to defend against escalade, the advantage to the attacker that cannon had briefly conferred was abruptly cancelled. As a result, after the 1520s, long and difficult sieges again became normal in European warfare wherever local authorities could afford the new style of fortification. Possession of a few big guns no longer sufficed to assure superiority over local defenses of any and every kind, as remained the case in other parts of the world.

Europe's continued political fragmentation meant that wars and preparations for wars continued to bulk very large in the public life of that part of the civilized world. A steady thrust after improvements in armament and military technique was one result. An elaborate and rapidly evolving art of war soon allowed European states to outstrip the gunpowder empires of Asia, where internal stimulus to improvement of armament design and military organization disappeared as soon as a single imperial center had effectually monopolized existing stocks of heavy artillery. As a result, by the eighteenth century or earlier, European land forces had attained a clear superiority over all rivals, matching the military superiority their ships had enjoyed from the time they first approached the shores of Asia.

There was still another aspect to Europe's political pluralism. No single sovereign could do much to subordinate mercantile and commercial activity to his own purposes. Taxation, if too heavy in one place, speedily led to flight of capital and trade to another location where costs of doing business were less. Hence, before the twentieth century, the autonomy of market-oriented activity vis-à-vis political command structures never came seriously into question.

The result was to maintain a far greater scope for market-regulated behavior in western Europe than was common in other parts of the civilized world. This in turn gave freer rein to the efficiency that private initiative and self-interest brought to the tasks of assorting and manufacturing goods and distributing services. Yet the rapid growth in the range and massiveness of market-regulated behavior did not prevent European command structures from also enhancing their power by creating more and more effective armies and navies. There is no need to underline the uniqueness of a situation in which the choice between guns and butter did not have to be made. The total wealth of western Europe rapidly increased, and in such a way that increases in taxation lagged far enough behind increases in wealth to allow spectacular expansion of privately owned and managed capital. Sung China had approached this condition too for a while, but private businessmen in China never won as much autonomy from their political superiors, nor accumulated capital on as large a scale, as European entrepreneurs managed to do in early modern times.

I would like to pause for a moment to emphasize how atypical the relationship between rulers and businessmen in western Europe really was. By about 1500, even the mightiest European rulers actually came to depend on traders and bankers for the means of organizing an efficient army. Instead of taxing away available wealth as was the norm in other civilized lands when military need asserted itself, western monarchs found themselves caught in the toils of private wheelers and dealers who insisted on making a profit on every transaction—or at least of seeing a good chance of making a profit. Rulers were actually unable to exert their sovereign power in war without soliciting loans from private persons who were usually domiciled beyond the bounds of the ruler's own jurisdiction and thus safe from confiscatory taxation. As early as the eleventh century in several important European cities, merchants became local sovereigns. Such city states offered initial havens for capital accumulation. Then, at a later time, in larger states like Holland and England, men whose wealth depended on buying and selling in the marketplace proved capable of defending themselves in war against indubitably legitimate political sovereigns who tried to assess new and burdensome taxes. This was, after all, a central issue in both the Dutch revolt of the sixteenth century and the English civil war of the seventeenth.

Many factors contributed to the autonomy that market-regulated behavior continued to enjoy in western Europe, and I do not mean to reduce everything to the survival of political pluralism. Still, it does seem to me that the European state system was crucial in preventing the takeover of mercantile wealth by bureaucratic authority in the way Chinese, Mughal, and Ottoman officials were able to do as a matter of course. In these imperial states, and in Spain as well, trade crossing jurisdictional borders fell into the hands of foreigners whose base of operation lay safely beyond reach of confiscatory taxation. Within the state itself, trade and manufacture was forced back toward retail and handicraft levels because any conspicuous concentration of capital (in anything other than land) swiftly attracted the tax collector's attention, making large-scale transactions on a private basis (except for tax farming) well nigh impossible.

Whenever government authorities wanted to concentrate resources—characteristically to equip and maintain an army—resort to compulsory corvée and levies in kind were necessary. Goods coming freely to market could not do more than sustain a retail supply of food and other necessary materials for city populations—and that, often, precariously.

By contrast, the growing power of European market-regulated behavior meant that larger and larger enterprises could be mounted by assembling goods and manpower in response to perceived private advantage. There was not, however, any simple dichotomy between public and private, bureaucratic and capitalistic management. On the contrary, private pursuit of profit and public administration could be and were merged by such bodies as the Dutch and English East India Companies, each of which came to exercise sovereign authority overseas. Indeed, as the scale of their operations increased, economic organizations aimed at private profit normally took on bureaucratic features that made them imperfectly distinguishable from governmental command systems. From the governmental side, European public officials often found it best to rely on market inducements when they sought to assemble the goods and services the sovereign authority required for its own purposes. Accordingly, corvée and other political ways of overriding spontaneous response to market incentives shrank in importance, though in practice compulsion was never entirely eschewed, especially when it came to recruitment into armies and navies.

The general effect, it seems obvious, was to improve the efficiency with which goods and services could be marshalled for large-scale undertakings. Amazingly, state power increased as compulsion diminished! Wealth increased as more massive and more mobile capital allowed new technologies, economies of scale, and interregional specialization to reinforce one another. In short, between the fourteenth and twentieth centuries, acceleration of Europe's capacity to produce wealth became autocatalytic—a self-sustaining process, perhaps best compared to the reaction of an atomic pile when one considers the disruptive consequences Europe's increasing wealth and power had for the rest of the world.

Within Europe itself, those states that gave the most scope to private capital and entrepreneurship prospered the most, whereas better governed societies in which welfare on the one hand or warfare on the other commanded a larger proportion of available resources tended to lag behind. After 1600, for example, Italian cities like Venice, where state policy protected the poor from the worst hardships of their condition, and militarized empires like those of Spain, Muscovy, and the Hapsburg cluster in central Europe all failed to keep pace with the economic development of such conspicuously undergoverned lands as Holland and England.

Diversification between a growingly powerful center and economically subordinated peripheral regions became a self-confirming, self-reinforcing pattern. Goods and services exchanged between center and periphery sustained continued growth of private capital at the center. This was so because toward the periphery the needs of the state were more clamant, taxation and bureaucratic regulation were more constricting, and skill remained in short supply. These differentials were also maintained by migration of entrepreneurs and of capital towards those central locations where conditions for making a fortune were most propitious. Sometimes, of course, private pursuit of wealth meant directing resources to distant places to start up mines or other new enterprises; more often it pulled entrepreneurs and capital towards a few urban centers in northwestern Europe where market exchanges were already most intense and where private wealth was already most secure against forcible expropriation.

All of these complex circumstances conducing to the expansion of European wealth and power were reinforced after the middle of the eighteenth century by what we are accustomed to refer to as the Industrial Revolution. Machinery using first water and then steam power cheapened goods enormously, allowing an increase of their quantity far beyond earlier possibilities. How drastic the result could be is well illustrated by a remark Robert Owen made in his *Autobiography* to the effect that cotton cloth costing half a guinea a yard in the 1790s could be purchased for two pence a yard in the 1850s—that is, for 1/63 of its earlier price. This makes it obvious why English manufacturers were able to undersell highly skilled Indian weavers on their own home ground by the early nineteenth century.

European merchants thus acquired a new weapon to upset existing social structures in other parts of the world in the form of a vast supply of goods that were far cheaper (and sometimes better) than anything that could be produced locally. Asian and African artisans suffered more directly. But change went far beyond the destruction of their prosperity: the sudden availability of new and cheaper goods, enlarged transportation capacities, and pressures to organize the production of raw materials and other goods that European merchants wanted to take in exchange for their proffered manufactures set the societies of all the rest of the earth into motion, often in ways that local rulers and old elites found distressing.

Yet efforts to check European economic penetration were seldom successful for long. Even in the eighteenth century, European states were ready and able to send armed forces to distant parts of the earth to support the interests of their merchants. In the nineteenth century, the technical equipment and disciplined art of war at the disposal of European expeditionary forces became overwhelmingly superior to arms and military organization available elsewhere. This became fully manifest in the 1840s when the British easily defeated Chinese defenders of Canton. The costs of such an action actually became trivial from the point of view of European state treasuries, committed, as they had been since the seventeenth century, to the maintenance of standing armies and navies. Hence the notorious "absence of mind" with which European empires expanded in the second half of the nineteenth century, until nearly all the globe had submitted to political as well as economic management from west European centers.

European imperialism was enormously facilitated by the fact that Europe's new surge of power arising from the Industrial Revolution coincided in time with what may be described as a "natural" rhythm of imperial decay in Asia. Gunpowder empires that had sprung into existence in the sixteenth and seventeenth centuries in the wake of the initial diffusion of cannon around the earth were all suffering from serious internal ailments by the late eighteenth century. Except in Japan, these empires had been founded by small warrior elites whose language and culture were alien to the great majority of their subjects. With time, the cohesion and military efficiency of such ruling groups diminished—the sweets of civilization being preferable to the hardships of military discipline. Governmental weakness and insecurity naturally resulted in both India and China. Another disturbing factor was the massive increase in peasant numbers, largely due to homogenization of infections. The result was to bring on a general crisis of Asian regimes so that by 1850 or so even the mightiest of them could offer only token resistance to European intrusion. Thus the extraordinary European world hegemony of the years 1850 to 1914 was partly illusory—a result of an accidental coincidence of Europe's new wealth and power with a period of exceptional weakness among Asian governments and ruling elites.

I should add, perhaps, that even though European rulers and state officials in the nineteenth century did not begin to sop up all of the new forms of wealth that burgeoned so luxuriantly in the lee of the Industrial Revolution, allowing private capital and levels of consumption to grow to unprecedented heights, still it was also true that new ideas and principles of political management expanded the range of public power over private citizens very greatly. For example, before the French Revolution, ordinary subjects had been immune from military service. From the upper classes, only volunteers entered armies and navies; conscription, which was needed to fill the lower ranks, was confined to specially disadvantaged classes of the population, such as the urban unemployed, landless peasants, merchant-seamen, and the like.

The French Revolution changed all that, making liability to military conscription the price of citizenship—at least for young males. Liberal revolution also swept away a multitude of privileged corporations and statuses that had previously limited the jurisdiction of state officials. By making everyone equal in law, everyone became equally free, and also equally liable to compulsory state service. For a few decades, the freedom arising from removal of older social barriers and differentiations was more apparent than the new subordination to centralized direction that liberal and democratic principles of government also implied. The potential for a political capture of the enhanced human and material resources the Industrial Revolution made available became apparent only in the twentieth century. This is, in turn, part of a larger readjustment whereby the recent decades of world history have begun to redress the exceptional lopsidedness of global relationships that worked so remarkably in Europe's favor between 1500 and 1900.

Taking the microparasitic side of things first, the central event of our time was the dramatic reduction of infant mortality, first in the Western world, then throughout most of the globe. This was due to the application of public health measures, beginning about 1850 but attaining a truly global scale only in our own time, mainly since 1945. Once medical researchers were able to decipher patterns of infection—the first human disease to be so deciphered was cholera, in 1884—cheap and effective ways of interrupting the chain of infection were soon devised: vaccination, pasteurization, hand washing, and the like. The childhood diseases of civilization ceased to matter very much when confronted by such countermeasures. Infants ceased to die in the old-fashioned way, with consequences well-known to worried demographers and ecologists. The resultant population explosions in Asia, Africa, and Latin America are fundamental disturbers of world balances today, and will remain so for some time to come.

Yet countervailing forces are not absent. Micro-organisms have a way of speedily circumventing medical and chemical attack, since their short life cycles allow rapid genetic change when some radically new selective pressure is brought to bear upon them. The recrudescence of malaria in regions where it was once thought to have been banished is perhaps the most important example of this tendency for natural balances to reassert themselves even in face of modern scientific techniques. Other kinds of disease, too, have arisen to replace the one-time formidable infectious diseases of childhood, although most of these manifest themselves mainly among adults—cancer, for example. Disease, in short, remains a significant factor in human ecology, despite the radical shifts in its incidence that the propagation of scientific medicine provoked during the last hundred years.

On the macroparasitic side, too, the extraordinary domination that market-regulated behavior enjoyed in Europe between the fourteenth and nineteenth centuries has clearly begun to meet with enhanced resistances. These arise partly from within the dominating societies, and on two levels. Most striking of these, perhaps, is the way in which corporations pursuing profit have themselves evolved from small-scale individual- or family-managed companies into bureaucratic command structures. Large business corporations do not respond internally to market direction in any very obvious way, even though managers are accustomed to measure their success in terms of a balance sheet derived from the "foreign" transactions such corporations may have made with other similar corporations as well as with governments and small-scale retailers. Managed prices set for transactions that occur within such corporations can often be extended to transactions with outsiders. This is especially true when the purchaser is a government (also bureaucratically organized) and when the goods or services offered for sale are such that only a few suppliers (or perhaps even a single supplier) can provide them.

This internal dynamic of capitalist organization was matched by the way in which converging considerations of warfare and welfare have led to pervasive public intervention in market processes. Here the great landmark was World War I (1914-1918), when men and things were mobilized on a scale and with a rigor undreamed of earlier. During this period, war and social welfare came to be closely linked: when munitions factories mattered as much as army divisions for winning the war, administrative measures designed to promote troop welfare could logically be expanded to apply to civilians as well. This was normalized during World War II (1939-1945), when all the major belligerents resorted to rationing and, almost inadvertently, thereby equalized access to many scarce commodities for rich and poor alike. War experience of state socialism was carried over into peacetime (especially during the economic depression of the 1930s) with varying degrees of rigor, depending on how effectively the prevailing political system mobilized lower-class aspirations for greater economic equality.

Resistance to the regime of the market also mounted in the peripheral regions of the earth where weakness and poverty of the past was widely resented by those peoples who had been compelled to submit to political or economic dependence. The critical landmark here, too, dates back to World War I, when Russian revolutionaries set out to repudiate the tyranny of the market in the name of justice, equality, and a more perfect freedom. In practice, Russian Communism owed more to patterns of war mobilization than to Marxist ideals, for Lenin and his heirs carried forward into peacetime and normalized the bureaucratic patterns of state socialism and manpower mobilization that had been invented in World War I.

It looks, therefore, as though our own age has witnessed a rapid readjustment of balance between market-directed and bureaucratically directed behavior that comes closer to what may properly be regarded as the civilizational norm—assuming that the behavior of most civilized states and peoples most of the time is the appropriate definition of the norm. If so, a probable consequence will be a fairly rapid slowdown of technical and other changes, for bureaucracies characteristically resist disturbances of routine and are powerful enough to make their distaste for innovation effective. Competition among rival states and among rival corporations is what now inhibits bureaucratic conservatism. Such competition may of course continue to push rival command systems to seek some advantage by ever-renewed efforts at technical and organizational change, but agreements to limit such efforts are likewise conceivable—either tacit or formalized into treaties (like SALT I and II) and cartels.

Indeed, it is easy to imagine a time not far in the future when existing public and private bureaucracies might come together into a self-perpetuating structure aimed first and foremost at keeping things as nearly stable as possible by guarding the privileges and power of existing managerial elites around the globe. If this should happen, market-regulated behavior will swiftly be cribbed, cabined, and confined to the interstices of society. This is exactly where it belonged in civilized state systems before 1000 A.D., when the modern expansion and eventual runaway explosion (seventeenth to nineteenth centuries) of market behavior began.

Such a vision of the past and future does not really suggest, however, that stability across long centuries lies ahead. Too many violent upheavals of ecological patterns have been set in motion by humanity's recent breakaway from older modes of life for even a very skilled managerial bureaucracy to navigate the future without confronting—perhaps often exacerbating—large-scale crises. Accessibility of cheap birth control devices means that recent population growth is quite likely to yield to population collapse, if young women reacting against their mothers' enslavement to the cradle cease to find the heavy task of nurturing infants worth their while. A pattern whereby in some parts of the world human reproduction falls below replacement levels while existing growth patterns persist elsewhere is even more probable for the near future—that is, across the next fifty to one hundred years. Such conditions will obviously set the scene for *Völkerwanderungen* of a massive kind, whether in the wake of wars or through individual and family migrations.

Raw material shortages are no less likely to harass our descendants in ways more severe than anything we have yet glimpsed in the form of petroleum supply difficulties. The industrial era of the past two hundred years may in retrospect appear to be the work of spendthrift generations who mined fuels and minerals recklessly and with consequences for natural balances that only millennia will be able to heal.

Humanity, in short, is not likely to run out of problems to confront nor of changes needing to be made in prevailing practices, even if market behavior—the main motor of recent social and economic change—should disengage from the driveshaft of global society. Action and reaction within a complex ecological web will not cease, and efforts to understand its functioning fully and to foresee future side effects will continue to elude human capacity for some time to come, and perhaps forever.

As long as these circumstances persist, stability will remain unattainable in human affairs, however much rulers and managers may desire it. Like all other forms of life, humankind remains inextricably entangled in flows of matter and energy that result from eating and being eaten. However clever we have been in finding new niches in that system, the enveloping microparasitic-macroparasitic balances limiting human access to food and energy have not been abolished, and never will be.

To emphasize that fact and to improve our understanding of humanity's revolutionary record within the web of life that spreads so precariously and magnificently over the earth's surface has been the goal and purpose of these lectures. If the vision of the human condition I impart seems gloomy, deterministic, and unattractive, I regret it. Personally I feel quite the opposite, finding a certain enlargement of the spirit in recognizing my own and all humanity's kinship with other forms of life, while also admiring the manner in which social interactions, symbolic meanings, and human intelligence have allowed an otherwise unimpressive species to transform the conditions of life over and over again—for ourselves, and for nearly all the other animals and plants that share the earth with us.

Surely the remarkable power of mind, of culture, and of the meaningful word to alter material processes is dramatically demonstrated by humanity's historic role in altering the face of the earth. In weaving these words together to make this presentation I, too, attest my lively faith in the power of words to alter the way human beings think and act. What we believe about the past, after all, does much to define how we behave in the present and what we do towards making up the future. If these lectures contribute even in a small way to improving the adequacy of our hindsight, I will be well pleased. Better hindsight deepens insight and makes for a less imperfect foresight. It thus improves the human condition, and to this, surely, we all aspire.

# Index

# Index

insects, plant parasites, 14
inventions, 9; in transportation, 19
Iran, 45
irrigation, 16, 17, 18, 52; economic
    effects of, 21; microparasitism
    and, 19
Islam, 32, 33; commercial de-
    velopment, 51–52; Italian rivalry
    for trade, 52, 53; merchants in,
    35–36
Italy, trade, 52, 53

Japan: Chinese trade with, 50, 52;
    consolidation of empire, 60, 67;
    European trade with, 56; pirates,
    47
Judaism, 33

Korea, Chinese trade with, 50, 52
Kushan empire, 41

landlords, 43–44, 46; merchants
    and, 43, 44
Lenin, Nikolai, 72

macroparasitic-microparasitic bal-
    ances, 8–10, 74
macroparasitism: in agriculture,
    17–18; in commercial transmuta-
    tion, 59, 70–72; definition of,
    6–8; in exploitative relations
    among human beings, 7–8, 10;
    urban transmutation and, 21–28;
    of warrior class, 22
malaria, 11*n*, 29, 70
Manichaeism, 33
market-regulated behavior (econ-
    omy), 9–10, 43, 53; in China,
    48–52, 54, 63; in commercial
    transmutation, 70–73; in Europe,
    and political pluralism, 61–64;
    European dominance of, 56
Marx, Karl, 4, 72
Mauryan empire, 24, 41

measles, 19–20, 24, 31
Mediterranean region, trade, 44,
    52–53
merchants, 48; distrust of, 35–37; in
    Industrial Revolution, 66–67;
    landlords and, 43, 44; rulers and,
    34–35, 42, 62–63
Mesopotamian civilization, 21, 28
microparasitism: in agriculture, 14,
    16–18; in commercial transmuta-
    tion, 31–32, 57–58, 69–70; defini-
    tion of, 6; European trade and,
    57–58; infant mortality reduced,
    69; in prehistory, 11–12; in urban
    transmutation, 19–25
Middle East: commercial de-
    velopment, 51–52; early agricul-
    ture in, 15–17; early civilizations
    in, 21–23; food supply, 58
military-bureaucratic manage-
    ment, 41–42
military service, conscription, 68
minerals, shortage of, 73–74
Ming dynasty, 60
Mohammed, 35–36, 47. *See also*
    Islam
money in China, Sung dynasty,
    48–50
Mongol empire, 48; China con-
    quered by, 51, 54; collapse of, 54
Mongol peoples, 47
Moslems, *see* Islam
Mughal empire, 60, 63
Muscovy, 60, 65
mutuality, 9
myxomyatosis of rabbits, 23*n*

Near East, *see* Middle East
nomads, 45–47; invasions by, 26,
    47. *See also* steppe cultures

occupational specialization, 18, 21
Ottoman empire, 60, 63
Owen, Robert, 66

# Index

Parthian empire, 41

peasants: in Asia, increasing, 68; in commercial transmutation, 44; distrust of merchants, 36; as majority, 8, 18, 43

Persian empire, 28

Philip II, King of Spain, 60

plague, bubonic, Black Death, 54. *See also* epidemics

plants: in early agriculture, 13-16; parasites on, 14, 16

Pleistocene epoch, 12-13

plowing, 16, 17, 21

Polo, Marco, 35, 52

population expansion: disease control and, 69-70; food production and, 58; prehistoric, 12, 14, 15

population stability: epidemics and, 27-28; prediction of, 73

Portugal: overseas empire, 60; trade with Asia, 55

prehistory: agriculture in, 13-16; hunting and gathering culture in, 11-13; microparasites in, 10-12; periods of, 3-4; population expansion in, 12, 14, 15

price fixing, 42

price system, 34, 43, 49

private enterprise, 64-66, 68; corporations, 70-71, 72; rulers and businessmen, 62-63

protein in diet, 46

rabbits, myxomyatosis, 23*n*

raiding and plundering, 7, 21-22, 26, 47

Ranke, Leopold von, 4

raw materials, shortage of, 73-74

religions: rise and spread of, 32-34; wars and, 33

rent and tax collection, *see* tax and rent collection

rice, productivity improved, 50

Roman Empire, 24, 28, 41; disinte-gration of, 31-32; late, trade, 44-45

rulers, 25; European, and businessmen, 62-63; merchants and, 42, 62-63; trade and, 45, 47. *See also* imperial command system

ruling class, 26-27; in China, 51; warriors, 21-22, 67-68

Russian empire, rival of Chinese empire, 59

Russian Revolution, 72

salt manufacture and distribution, 51

Sargon I of Akkad, 24

schistosomiasis, 19

sewage, 19

ships, 29-31, 42, 44, 50

Siberia, 58

Silk Road, 54

Sinkiang, 45

slash and burn cultivation, 16

smallpox, 19, 24, 31

Smith, Adam, 49

social welfare and wars, 71

South China Sea, 50

Southeast Asia, 28, 53

Spain, 65; overseas empire, 60

spice trade, 53, 55

state socialism, 71, 72

steppe cultures, 26, 28, 46; horses and cavalry in, 46, 59; plague in, 54; trade, 45-46, 54

Sung dynasty, 48, 49, 62

Syria, 29

tax and rent collection, 7, 17, 25-27, 30, 36; in China, 48-50; trade related to, 43, 45

taxation in Europe, 63-65

tax farming, 51, 63

technology, 65; Chinese, 50, 51; in Dark Ages, 33; in war, 60-61

Tigris-Euphrates valley, 16-17

THIS BOOK WAS PRINTED ON 60 LB. WARRENS OLDE STYLE
AND SET IN 10 ON 12 V-I-P BEMBO. THE ROMAN IS AN IN-
TERPRETATION OF A TYPE CUT BY FRANCESCO GRIFFO OF
BOLOGNA FOR ALDUS MANUTIUS OF VENICE AND WAS FIRST
USED IN A TREATISE BY PIETRO BEMBO IN 1495. THIS BOOK
WAS EDITED BY CATHY DAMMEYER,
DESIGNED BY BRUCE CAMPBELL,
AND PRINTED BY PRINCETON
UNIVERSITY
PRESS